Wind Whispers

A Poetry Anthology

Debbie Quigley

Wind Whispers

A Poetry Anthology

Debbie Quigley

ISBN-13: 978-1502736376

ISBN-10: 1502736373

Copyright©2014 Debbie Quigley. All rights reserved. No part of this publication may be reproduced, distributed, or transmitted in any form or by any means, including photocopying, recording, or other electronic mechanical methods, without the prior written permission of the author.

DEDICATION

In memory of my husband, David Michael Quigley.

CONTENTS

Introduction..7

Wind Whispers..9

When You Want to Cry..11

Life's Choices..12

I Believe..13

October Campfire...15

The Mask I Wore..17

The Cost of an Addict.. 19

God Wiped Away the Other Tear..21

Moms Lessons..23

Daddy's Hand...26

Dear Husband of Mine..29

Love Memories...32

When You Think of Me..36

Promise 39

Thank You Lord..41

Just a Dream...43

Memorable Magic Moment...45

My Glass Room of Solitude...48

Winter Sight..51

Two Gentle Giants..53

My Tapestry of Life	57
Can I Sit With You?	59
Woman's Whisper	62
The Lord Picked Up My Hand	64
Winds of Change	66
Visit to the North on Dec 24	68
Hour Glass of Emotions	70
Sometimes I Cry	75
Lost Heart	77
Someday Dreams	79
My Loves	81
The Pen	84
Canadian Winter Walk	87
Angel Wing Songs	89
Who Are You?	91
Wind Whisper Journey	93
Time Is	98
Wind Whispers Finale	101
Author Biography	103

Introduction

Wind Whispers is about baring life's crosses.

With faith and hope, things improve and those crosses get lighter.

Love is a powerful emotion that can build you up or tear you down. This book will open your heart to a belief in love.

Love always gives hope that all is not lost.

If you have no faith or question whether you should have to help you with today's life filled with problems, this book is for you!

Come along with me as I guide you through some wind whispers.

No matter what you are going through in life, I believe that miracles do happen.

I share with you miracles and strength received in my own personal life. Life has sent me many smiles along with a river of tears. I started writing to help others one reader at a time.

I open my heart to you filled with many lessons of hope, love and courage. Faith and the love of nature helped me through my darkest moments.

Nature helped in many ways to bring back the peace I once held in my heart.

Take my hand walk with me. Things will get better as you will see no matter what life has handed you through loss there is also miracles!

You will find the strength to move forward through grief, loss and find the courage to be happy once again. Allowing nature to be part of your healing it was helpful to me I know it will help you also!

As I take you on a poetic path of life, your job is to open your heart to life's many possibilities!

Wind Whispers

Love for today and hope for another day.

A forgiving heart for the ones you love

God answers prayers from up above

Faith to believe in messages from loved ones gone.

They send messages of love and sometimes a song.

A feather, butterfly for you to see

Trust, in your heart, the messages it receives

I have come to believe in a Higher Power above

Also in angels that are filled with love

Open your heart for the world to see

Include nature's beauty in your plight

It will cleanse your soul and change your life.

As you read on, you will see the miracle

Important lessons that I gained through life.

Dealing with love, losses, heart-ache and strife in my life.

That helped me believe I call them wind whispers.

Faith, hope, courage and strength that I attained on life's journey

I now pass on my whispers to help you to carry on with a dream

Whatever you are going through you are not alone!

Enjoy this book with all my love!

When You Want to Cry

When you feel like you could cry

Remember the bird's song

That each new season is a change in time

Each new day like a new banner in the sky

It is a day to reflect that each tear

Leads to a new lesson learned

Each bad day offers an opportunity to appreciate

The many good ones to come

So remember these things

When you feel like you could cry!

Life's Choices

Life is a song unsung

A play not performed,

An untold story

Life can be full of magic,

A script not yet written

You are the performer,

The writer the magician, in your life.

Make your choices so life

Can be the best song,

The finest play,

The most enriching story,

The most magical act

It can be everything you make it to be!

I Believe

I believe in you

I believe in me

I believe in us

I believe in love

I believe in honesty

I believe in trust

Things in common that brought

Us together

To live, love, laugh

Together sharing things in common

Interests and goals

Values we were raised with,

Things we trusted in,

We need to get back to all those things

We both believed to be true.

We need to be friends, lovers,

Companions again.

Our relationship needs to recover

From the things it is now lacking

It is worth saving, I believe!

Do you believe?

October Campfire

It was a warm October's day coming to an end

I started a campfire and looked at the grey blue sky

The trees lined up at the back lot

To meet the towering sky

The call of the blue jay, crickets fall songs,

Music to my ears I felt the thick carpet

Of grass, so soft and long.

My campfire was starting to burn.

The logs turned from brown to grey,

On this October day

Flames danced, the fire snapping,

Crackling as the wood turned to orange coals

The warmth on my legs felt so good

The smells from the burning logs

Wrapped me in comfort, warmed my soul.

My fire a beacon in the sky,

A light to ward off the night's darkness

I sat alone in the stillness,

Hearing the good-bye cries of the loons.

On this October night,

I pondered how quickly summer had come and gone,

Knowing too soon it would all be over

The seasons end!

The Mask I Wore

I wore a mask to hide the pain

Praying daily that things would change

A smile I wore even though

My heart was filled with fear.

I wore a false smile, year after year,

To try and hide many a tear

Believing I was alone in my plight

Hoping my adult child would wake up

And see the light!

When I uncovered my mask

For all the world to see

I found out there were a Millions of Mothers

Who wore their masks

Just like me!

I am no longer wearing the mask of pain

I will not feel alone again!

Dedicated to the Mothers whose secret they hide. You are not alone!

The Cost of an Addict

True friends gone

Family estranged

Mothers' tears and heartbreak

Broken trusts with siblings

Loyalty to family gone

Pride of oneself gone

Society's laws disobeyed,

God's laws broken

The high cost to be an addict!

Is high!

The cost to keep living as one

Or to die!

Being in jail as one!

The costs of an addict are high

Are they worth it?

A lifetime of highs to you?

Dedicated to Chris...God is helping him stay clean and sober.

God Wiped Away the Other Tear

It was a cold, crisp day in February

Two trucks and a head on crash

That changed me and my family

Since that day, looking back

Raven lying in a coma

Between here and Heaven's gate

Only God knew her fate

The doctors believed

She might not come back

If she did her brain

Might not be on track

We continued prayers

Both day and night

A miracle my son did see

Raven awoke from her coma state

One tear rolled down her cheek

The Lord had determined her fate

He wiped away her other tear

It is a miracle she is here!

We will never forget that one tear!

Thanks be to God

Raven is here!

Dedicated to Raven Holloway
Mother of my Granddaughter Emerald Marshall

Moms Lessons

I learned from her to be strong

To work hard or nothing would be gained

Hold your head up high

Be a lady with some grace

Mom always had a joke to tell

A smile upon her face

Be kind to others she would say

What goes around comes back around

Will get you in the end!

Live life with dignity

Always keep your pride

Strive to be the best you can be

At whatever job you do

Always be honest and true

You have to live by the choices you make

In everything you do!

Never tell a lie as they cannot be remembered

After a day or two!

Will someday come back on you!

I am my Mothers daughter

Learned my lessons well

She now holds a place in Heaven

Still keeping her eye on me

I have lived my life in such a way

I know she was proud of me

Mom taught me all these lessons

I passed on to children of mine

Say prayers at night thank the Lord above

For the many blessings each and everyday

Always remember to help a stranger along the way

I am my Mothers daughter

Was so proud to be!

When my time is over here

I know she will be with me

Mom will take my hand

Will be together someday in Heavens promise land!

Till then will cherish special memories

Written in memory of Enid Seabrooke

DEBBIE QUIGLEY

Daddy's Hand

A hazel eyed man gazed down

At his little bundle of joy

Chubby cheeks eyes of blue starred back

He reached his large hand down in the little bed

A tiny little hand reached up

She grabbed a finger from the large hand

The years went by quickly

Skipping along holding that strong hand

Next thing it was pictures at the prom

Seemed like in the blink of an eye

The little girl was almost as tall as the man

It was a beautiful summer's day

The man held her hand

One last time!

He walked her down the aisle

Now a grown woman dressed in white

They stopped in front of the large crowd

He took what once was his baby daughter's hand

Placed it in the hand of another man

She whispered I love you Dad!

He whispered back I love you to!

As he walked away a tear rolled down his cheek

The bride never forgot that first man's hand

A few years later

A grey haired man stood over baby's bed

He reached his large hand down

God's little gift grabbed his finger

Baby's Mother stood beside the man

Whispering in his ear

I love you Dad!

The little angel starred back

At the grey haired man

Just like yester year

The little one grabbed his finger once again

The first hand in a little girl's life!

Daddy's Hand!

Dedicated in memory to my Dad Vern Seabrooke and my son Cory Marshall
It takes a special man to be a Dad!

Dear Husband of Mine

How I wish for a peaceful day

My head now spins like a ferris wheel at the local fair

Tears come and go like a spring with no end

Dear husband of mine you have gone to the Heavens

Without saying good-bye!

My heart aches for an understanding of why?

I told you not to leave me alone

The smile I have to wear daily hiding the pain

Pain of loss and sorrow has engulfed me

Like huge waves that crash to the shore

My heart yearning for direction struggling daily

Trying to put life in order once more

My strength to fight is slowly subsiding

Trust of friends gone like a balloon in the sky

Working and working to hang onto what we worked for

Keeping my pride to struggle ahead and move forward

Friends have had their hands out since you have been gone

It is a nightmare without an end!

Feeling lost in a dark tunnel not knowing which way to turn

I trust in good time there will be light

Light that will put peace in my heart

Never will I trust the same again

I pray each night to the Heavens above

Asking for help to cope each day

All I ask for is a peaceful day!

A day to enjoy the stars at night

Flowers for my eyes once again to see

I want back to that place of peaceful serenity

Still in shock that you are gone!

Dear husband of mine!

My husband passed away April 6 2013 many poems are written in his memory.
I have written a few poems sharing with you the grief of this loss.
We all believe that will have tomorrow but tomorrow is not promised.
My husband was only 57 years old God took him home early.
Tell your loved ones every day that you love them!

Remember Dave's legacy!
Tomorrow is not promised!

DEBBIE QUIGLEY

Love Memories

When I met you I thought you were the one

That special man I prayed for when in the dark of night

You came into my life at mid- life

My soul mate I thought from the start

Now you are in Heaven

I am all alone!

I thought you were with me to stay

Until we grew old and grey

We had something special you and me

There is a soul mate for everybody

You were the one for me!

May 4 2001 was a memorable day

All vows taken seriously with all of my heart

We never fought like couples do

Believed our love would last forever

Thought we would never part

You were all I wanted for many years

I would have never dreamed

Trust was broken vows taken torn apart

My heart was shattered in pieces

I decided to leave our home

I thought leaving our home would make you change your ways

Hoped you would reach out and say" Let's try again how about you come home to stay."

Instead God reached out his hand early and took you straight home

There was so many things I wanted to say

Most important was the love I had for you

I know we will meet in Heaven

Maybe you will tell me

That you never stopped loving me!

Your smile is implanted in my heart

Your gentle spirit blue eyes that seemed to twinkle in the dark

I loved you from the very start

Sorry was not given

No options asked on where you wanted to be

Family made the choices not me!

I would have taken you to the home we once shared

Choices were made excluding the love

I had for the many years we shared before we parted

Sadness does not convey the feelings in my heart

I loved you the memories will stay

In a special place inside my heart

You will always be the man that held my heart

Clear blue skies are your eyes

Gentle rains are the tears that flow

Flowers and veggie plants are my gifts to you

Please hold my hand and help me

To make it through

You were my man of strength

I once trusted with my heart

Please help me to remember the love we once shared

Don't forget to look down from the Heavens

Maybe send me a rainbow or maybe even two!

So I know you are watching from the Heavens

You have left this earth but really are not gone

If not a rainbow a feather a song for you to share!

DEBBIE QUIGLEY

When You Think of Me

Think of the sweet smell of a bouquet of fresh flowers

A campfire crackling with hot coals

A warm hug on a cold night

A lesson or two I taught you

Think of the love of nature

A gentle summer breeze

A clear blue sky

Or a moon lite night

When you think of me

Think of the love for trees

And for the Lord above

Disney movies and gentle rains

When you think of me I will be there for you!

One More Day

I just wanted one more day

That I could hold your hand

One more day to tell you

I missed you being around

But stresses of life tore us apart

That was not our plan on the start

We all say things we do not mean

I loved you from the very start

Things got in the way and broke my heart!

One thing you taught many

Is say what you need to say!

We like to think a tomorrow is in site

We never know when the Lord

Will take our hand and guide us to the light

Do not leave things unsaid

Tell your loved ones every day!

Sometimes we are not given one more day!

As we are only promised today!

Love
Debbie

One More Day written April 8 2013
In memory of husband Dave Quigley passed April 6, 2013

Promise

Promise is any easy word to say

I promise to do something

People say everyday

If you promise to do something

Let it be a word of honor

Not just something that you say

Promises held are important

Just like handshakes were back in the day

Never promise anything lightly

Like promise to love only you

Take a vow and promise it to be true

A promise from a loved one is believed to be true

Not just something to say the same

As I love you I do I do!

If you need to break a promise

Tell the person you made it to

As promises should not be broken

Unless honesty is involved too!

Thank You Lord

Thank you for the joys you have put into my heart

The birth of my sons and precious Granddaughter

Thank you for giving me the most wonderful Mother

That helped in creating the woman I am today

Thank you for allowing me to give back to her some of the gifts

Of happiness of friendship and undying love she gave me

Thank you for my Dad he taught me and understanding of alcoholism.

But for the grace of God go I!

Teaching me the Serenity Prayer which is my favorite to this day

My husband for the lessons he taught me

Sharing with me the simple things in life that God provides

Nature, deer, rivers and streams flowers and growing veggies

Simple life dreams!

Gentle friendship we shared for a few years

Thank you Dave for the gold band that meant so much to me

Thank you for being a part of my life on our special day in May

Thank you for the friends over the years that have come and gone in my life.

Friends that taught me the gifts that I did not believe I possessed

Friends that hurt me and broke my heart

Lessons that made me trust what instincts tell also empathy

I know the feeling from a broken heart

Thank you for the calling to be a caregiver to the old

The abundance of love that they return

Thank you for answering my prayers as the years have past

Holding my hand when others had left

Thank you Lord for my 57th year!

Just a Dream

As I sat looking out the window

The white airy flakes fell from the Heavens

The winds gently blew the small flakes to and fro

Landing on the sun glistened white grounds below

The tree branches catching the white blanket

They now wore their sweaters of white

The icicles hanging from the roofs edge

Pointed swords of different lengths

Shining winter crystals that catch the light

Snowflakes join forces with the wind

The snow gusts in circles while in flight

Swiftly over the backyard and over the trees

Images are fading from my window pane

I woke up in my chair it was dark at night!

Wrapped in my lace sweater!

On this cold winters night!

DEBBIE QUIGLEY

Oh it was just a dream!

Memorable Magic Moment

It was June 2014 much had changed in this so called life

I was back in the small hamlet a place of solitude to me

The sun was warm on my skin felt like a Mothers touch

Blue jay cries and robins chirped loving the warm rays of the sun

A gentle breeze caressed my locks

A love touch feeling that I have not felt in so long

Large windmill flowers spinning around and around

Long grasses wild flowers swayed in the gentle breeze

I was here in peaceful paradise

That I call home again!

Daily dragonflies fly like helicopters overhead

My heart is still my lungs filled with fresh air

Sky is blue with streaks of clouds above

Mindfully crafted each cloud unique in shape and design

Mixture of tree top branches meet the sky

I sat pondering how blessed this moment is to me

The simplicity of nature's sounds is all my ears here

A hummingbird whizzes by to the sugary water drink delight

Yellow buttercups and daisies entwined in the long grasses

Shadows on the tree lined wall lends the many shades of green

My heart beats slow as my eyes are open wide to memorable magic

Simplicity bountiful on this day

The moments engulf my heart with the love of what is before me

Love that wrapped around me while on sat in my chair

A feeling of happy contentment at last

In 2012 closed my eyes in a dream

Picturing the winter scene from my mind

Of the place I once called home

Today's moment thankfully is not a dream

A summer's day that will fill my heart day after day

I am home at last!

Each day that passes in my life memorable moments

They give me comfort healing

What once was a shattered heart

Magic of these summer moments have healed my heart

Appreciating nature at its finest

At my little piece of heaven in the North

I thank God each day for these blessed moments

Memorable moments on a summer's day!

My Glass Room of Solitude

I sit in my room of solitude, my favorite place to be

One comfy chair covered in a tapestry

Trimmed on the edges pictures of houses and trees

One artificial cherry tree full of pink blooms

A long shelf covered with a white cloth

Holds things that give comfort to me

A ceramic angel clock with old numbers on its face

Sounds its reliable tick tock, tick tock

The fire crackles as I sit in my glass room

A shamrock and prayer plant lends colour

Against the panes of glass

A small electric candle light

Casts a pink hue in the dark of night

Beside the chair rests a square wicker basket

That holds my journal and a pen or two

Looking out through my glass panes

I see the smoke billowing from the chimney

On this brisk winter's day

I am cozy and warm

A carpet beneath my feet

With colours of maroons and greys

The snow banks piled high

My angel statue her wings

Are all that can be seen

The California blue spruce tips covered in white mittens

The large pine branches sag to meet the snow banks below

Across the road, the tree branches charcoal crosses on a white page

Snowflakes slowly descend now from the Heavens

It is quiet and still as I look out from my glass room of solitude

I appreciate nature's beauty continually changing beauty

Each day brings something different to the scene for me

It is a day of comfort and thankfulness

DEBBIE QUIGLEY

For my small room of glass and the comfort it gives me!

Winter Sight

Gentle dusting of snow flakes falling from the heavens,

Floating endlessly, dancing in many directions

Before landing on the snow covered grounds below

Pine trees laden with winter's blast of snow

Their branches heavy like stiff arms in the harsh cold

Icicles droop from the roof top

Like crystal swords,

Their ridges oh- so - perfect in design

The points drip slow water drops to meet

The new fallen snow

The air is clean, crisp

Nothing is moving

All is still

The snowflakes gently whisper

Around my head

The backyard, a backdrop of white

Sunshine rays on the trees

Casting their shadows

Snow banks are piled high like mountain tops

Their peaks rounded by last night's winds blast

Each has its artistic role to play

In creating nature's wondrous scenes

The snow, wind, sunshine and the trees

Join forces in creating nature's designs of this beautiful winter sight!

Two Gentle Giants

The Lord sent two gentle giants into my life

When it was full of heartache and strife

My husband left for the Heavens without saying good-bye

Leaving debts and everything unfinished

Stress of what to do next seemed to keep piling high!

A mountain I did not know how to climb

My trust in humanity was dead and gone

I did not know which way to turn

What do I tackle first as a woman all alone!

A gentle giant came into my life

Reminding me there are people

Who just want to help a wounded soul!

Helping them pick up broken pieces in life

To move forward with a helping hand

My little piece of Heaven feared

Would have to give up on my dream

Retiring in the peaceful North

My gentle giant friend

Opened my heart to the possibility

That all is not lost for my house in the North

Larry introduced me to another angel giant

Paul worked on the plumbing without a big bill

Was shocked when the Lord's giant shook my hand

Little gas money was all he would take

Then shook my hand and wished me the best!

Loaded up his truck have not seen him since that day

This gentle giant did not know me from a whole in the ground

A best friend of Larry my giant friend

I believe the Lord had sent me

The Lord sent me two giants

When I talked looked up to

Reminding me there are kind souls

Still left in this world that just want to help a wounded soul

Giving light to another

So their dreams can be fulfilled

A stream of light came to me that day

Giving me light to face everyday

Moving ahead towards my simple life dreams

I now know that I will live in the North again

That I will not allow anybody to hurt me again

I am a small woman but can manage on my own

Learning things from my gentle giant friend

My little piece of Heaven in the North

Is slowly coming back to the place I will call home

I have learned many lessons since that day

Have realized I cannot shut down my heart

These gentle giants taught me there are people

Still left in this world that do things to help another

Bending down to lend a helping hand

I have grown so much since that day

The large mountains I had to climb

Now just little mounds to step over

Each day and month that passes by

Continued path of my life- long dream

I picked up my pen once again

I am a writer touching hearts

With poetry since that day

I like the gentle giants Larry and Paul

They put light back in my soul

A light that I now pass on

With courage and strength

To never give up on a dream!

Written in dedication to Larry Bertrand and Paul Pilon

My Tapestry of Life

As the rain fall from the Heavens

Like the tears held in my heart

Another day another month gone

The Heavens opened the gates

To welcome my husband home

The gardener

He will take his large hands

Creating gardens for the angels to see

I now take life with a simple approach

Without a plan

Wanting now to just enjoy

Simple pleasures once again

I like the flower cannot unfold my life

Wanting and controlling only God's hands

Like my husband's hand could not unravel what was to be

I am where I am today!

Who knows about tomorrow!

I trust the Lord will help me along

Each day like gold thread enter twined into a tapestry

Nobody knows the outcome of our tapestry of life

The end of the tapestry design

Is the end of one's life

Tapestry filled with love

Growth of wisdom lessons attained

My tapestry filled with love for my children and Granddaughter

Love for seniors I care for

The deer, trees and friends

Encased in my tapestry of golden threads

Of days of yester years past

At mid-life loving natures beauty

God provides for free

Opening my heart to new possibilities for my tapestry of life!

Can I Sit With You?

I know you do not know my name

Can I sit with you?

When I look into your eyes

I also see your tear stained face

I want you to know whatever you are going through

You are not alone!

The Lord is watching over you and will help guide you through

Whatever is making your heart heavy and making you feel blue

I have also had so many trials believe I would not make it to

Sometimes you have to reach out even though it is hard to do

A few years back was crying from a broken heart

My neighbours said a prayer for me

Gave me the strength to get up off my knees

Now I am here for you and I do not know

What you are going through

But trust me the Lord turns the darkest moments

Of our lives to much needed light

I am older now have learned many lessons

That I can pass to you!

In this journey we call life

Your prayers will soon be answered

Sit back let me hold your hand

You are not alone

I will be your friend

Now you know my name

The Lord answered my prayers

Yours will be answered to!
Now you know my name we can be friends to!

I wrote this poem when in a depressed state after many losses feeling very much alone.

There are so many times during life's journey that you feel alone.
I have felt this many times holding my emotions inside.
Hiding my tears inside telling everybody all is well.
Reach out to a friend or family member or a stranger for that matter.
People need to express their pain and let it out!

Reach out help another that is why we are here to learn to grow.
Compassion costs nothing to give away!
Depression has become very prevalent in today's society.
It is a silent killer effecting both young and old depression has no boundaries.

Written in memory of Paul Vanin a beautiful young man
Paul now resides in heaven leaving behind his children.

Woman's Whisper

I am a woman of faith

I am a woman of grace

Strong and wise

Through life's lessoned learned

I can be whatever

I choose to be

With passion and persistence

Life can be full of hopes and dreams

The key is to never let go

Of the strength inside of you

Remember the lives of women

You came from

That challenged all odds

To give courage to women

Whatever colour, race or cause

If you have a dream

Keep climbing to achieve it

Don't ever let it go

This is the whisper

I want to share with you

We as women need to help

Each other no matter what

In every country and city

Encouraging each other

Passing on this whisper

So women everywhere

Will have the courage

Power and strength

To change whatever

In their lives

To make their dreams come true

This is my woman's whisper

With love I pass to you!

The Lord Picked Up My Hand

Placed a pen between my fingers

For ink to touch each page

To share parts of life I lived through to this stage

The pen writes of happiness and sad moments to

Giving strength to others when reader is feeling blue

Maybe after reading something dries a tear or two

So they do not feel alone along life's journey and long path

Hope a little light gets deep within another's heart

When the Lord put the pen in my hand

The words flow down unto the page

They are my deepest feeling directly from my heart

The Lord opened up my heart to share poems

Stories from my writing start

I write about nature for the people that do not get out

To take them to a place of beauty that I can still see

I am grateful to the Lord above for giving this gift to me!

Writing makes me happy deep down in my soul

I share with others to open hearts of other possibilities

The Lord picked up my hand and I started to write

Will continue to help others with my writing

That is my plight till the Lord shuts out my light!

The Lord made me a writer

When he put the pen in my hand

My greatest love

Is a piece of paper and pen in my hand!

Winds of Change

I am a year older

My husband has passed

I trust my instincts

Like never before

I cannot keep looking back

There is no returning to what once was

All I trust in is the Lord above

I trust the Lord

My beacon of light

I am here for a reason

Prayers keep me strong

I am here today

I must carry on!

I am here today!

Today is all that is promised

I will carry on!

Through the winds of change

The good Lord willing

There will be another day

To carry on!

With courage

Through life's winds of change

As we are not promised one more day!

Visit to the North on Dec 24

My anticipated drive to the North

The pines lined the road

Snow banks piled high

Sky was blue the air crisp and fresh

The sun dazzled the eyes

Millions of crystals on top of nature's winter blast

The snow fluffy and light

Little piece of heaven hiding

Behind the tall pines

Snow piled high

Little white house like a picture

From an old Christmas theme

Oh what a day of joy it brought me

Returning to the land of peaceful serene

Looking at winter beauty all around

A small doe jumped high in her heels

Leaps and bounds as she crossed the road

After plowing and shoveling three feet of snow

Sandwiches on pumpernickel bread tasted so good

Cold nipping our fingers noses red like Rudolf's

It was warm and cozy in the little white house

Looking out in the world of white

Icicles swords were the fringes

That hung from the top of the window panes

My heart felt warm as I sipped hot tea

Returning for a visit to my little piece of heaven on Dec.24th

DEBBIE QUIGLEY

Hour Glass of Emotions

I sat sifting through this year

Contemplating the tears of sadness

Another loved one from my life gone

Smiles of courage once again

Acceptance of valuable lessons learned

Each emotion runs through my mind

Slowly like each grain of sand as it trickles

Down the hour glass

Thankful for the blessings

Strength and hope received from God almighty

Proud of self for growth attained

I conclude I am stronger like the winds that cross the ocean

My heart of mixed emotions accepting the pain

I am wiser!

Surrendering the control of life's plan

I now take my life day to day

Thankful for each moment

That comes my way

Letting go of what once was

Growing into the mature woman

I am!

The Lord held my hand

Gave me the courage to write with a passion

In my heart to share

I am a healthcare worker

My calling to give light to seniors

Make their days a little brighter

I am a Mother and Grandmother

Full of life's journey and lessons

That need to be shared

I withstood the storm of life's challenges

Grasping for strength

In my hour glass of emotions

That slowly trickle down

Sifting through my mind

Each and every grain

My continued mixed emotions

Of my year up till now

A stronger wiser woman

I am today!

Life's wind whispers

Holding on through loss

Courage and hope given

I march on life's path

Grateful for the journey

The Lord has given me

Not always what I expected

Life is full of hour glass emotions

I am thankful thoughts run through my mind

I am grateful for happy memories

I am here!

I am me!

Darkest before the dawn

It soon will be a new year

During the winter

Time to contemplate growth

Accomplishments made

Lessons attained

Before the arrival of new

Spring a time of new growth

We are here to learn and grow

I am thankful for today

Yesterday and tomorrow

If it comes

Life's wind whispers

Hour glass of emotions

Sifted through!

Sometimes I Cry

When the rain falls

My heart opens to

Let the tears fall

Sometimes I cry

Remembering my loved ones past

Sometimes I cry when a hug is shared

The end of a movie of love between two

Sometimes I cry at the end of a song

Sometimes I dance alone in the dark

Tears of the dances shared

Sometimes I cry with tears

Of joy when something

Puts a light in my heart

A hug from an old friend from the past

Sometimes I cry to let out

What I hold inside

Tears of joy, sadness and pain

Sometimes I Cry

Thankful for God's love inside

The tears of sadness wiped away

Sunshine to dry the tears

Facing another day

Family, friends shared events

The tears hold many things

But most of all the sign that I am a living thing

One that feels, loves with all that a heart gives!

Lost Heart

A heart beats with sadness

The grip of loneliness

Missing the shared look between two

A love of a lifetime cut short

Trust and hope for a tomorrow

A silver lining of a time healed heart

Promises made of growing old together

Gone like the leaves off a tree in fall

A glimpse of sunshine starting to poke through

Pride keeping me upright as my heart beats on

Dark clouds have surrounded me since

Your departure a shock that you were gone

Lost heart it is time I let you go!

Acceptance that sometime we will meet again

Young hearts never understand the pain

The undying ache for a loved one gone

My lost heart will beat on

I will hold onto the path of my life's journey shared with you

A special place deep within my heart

There will always be a memory that reminds me of you!

Someday Dreams

Someday is a popular word

A word that holds our dreams

It is used often in adult society

When we are young we have many someday dreams

As far as someday dreams are concerned

But as we age we put our someday dreams off

Until someday never comes if we meet an early end

Turn your someday dreams into now dreams

Don't leave until evermore!

Make someday dreams come true

Take that trip, write a book

Make your heart sing!

Don't leave until tomorrow

As tomorrow is unclear

So I started on a someday plan

Someday I will have lots of flowers

Of every shape and size

My someday dream is in the works

The bulbs are in the ground

They will poke their little heads up

After winters long end

My yard will have lots of flowers!

Blooming until summers end!

My Loves

Happy memories in the past

Writing a poem a story to share

The smell of cedar and pine

Relaxing sent of lavender lingering around

The glow of candles in the dark

A million stars on a moon lite night

The smell of wood burning in the air

Campfire sounds of crackling wood

The twinkling colours of the hot coals

A full moon shining through the glass panes

White tailed deer in my backyard with a fawn or two

Fresh clean scent of clothes when removing from the clothes line

The warmth on my face on a summer's day

Picking fresh tomatoes off the vine

The wild rose bush in full bloom

Trees wearing their fall colours

The cry of the loons at night

Flowers of all colours shapes and sizes

A hot bath in bath salts

Laughter shared between my sons

My Granddaughters hugs

Smiles on faces of seniors

Having the right answers

Sitting at the lake

When it is calm and the mirror images

Reflections that can be seen

Birds and dragonflies flying overhead

Butterflies gliding flower to flower

A meal shared with a friend

The warmth of the house

When coming in from the cold

Picturesque beauty of trees covered in snow

Life is full of many loves

These are the ones

That make my heart sing!

Take the time to engulf your heart

In the loves that make your heart sing!

DEBBIE QUIGLEY

The Pen

The pen is an animate object that holds blue liquid in its veins

It helped write on paper about hopes and dreams

It helped if there is something you wanted to remember

The pen helped in writing it all down

The pen has come a long way in colour and design

It comes in all colours not used like in the past

I think of years ago a feather pen one would hold unto

Dip it in the ink bottle for their story to be told

The pen put down on paper love letters to behold

Sometimes the pen wrote words on paper

That never should never have been told

Once hurtful words are on paper they cannot be taken back

You cannot erase words the pen helped write once they are sent

The pen helped people write down all of their desires

The pen helps the words flow down unto the page

Then a letter was sent

The pen helped write many good-bye letters

Or love letters in the past

Sometimes the ink on paper would make another smile

Words written on paper a lesson would be learned

Today the pen is not used as much replaced

With a finger and a computer pad

A phone or text a message is futures way to write

No matter how you write a message

That you send make sure it does not hurt

The person that receives it at the other end

We use now the tip of our finger

For our words to be received

It does not matter what you use

Some words are best expressed in person

Think about the words you write

Are they words you would want to read?

If not do not press send!

E-mail a text message to a friend

Make sure it is something

You would want to read if on the receiving end!

Canadian Winter Walk

On a cold winters day stepped out into the cold

My furry blue hat keeping my ears from freezing cold

The cold air I felt travelling down to my lungs

Cold winter winds nipping at my nose and down to my toes

As I took each step in my warm winter boots

The crackling sounds as I took each step in the new fallen snow

The blue sky overhead filled with clouds of white

Lends colour to the world below

The trees wearing their white mittens

I walked on swinging my arms walking on this winters day

My coat crackling as my arms swung at my sides

The vision of smoke billowing from chimneys as I looked straight ahead

The cars passed by slowly with clouds following behind

I walked on the birds not singing too cold to make bird sounds

The squirrels in their leaf homes high off ground

My cheeks pinched from the winter's cold

I remember the feeling from many winters past

The appreciation for the warmth of a home

The sounds of the crackling and snapping from the cold

Were the only sounds I kept hearing while walking home

Home at last I opened the door meeting the warmth of the air

I will now sit down and enjoy my hot cup of tea

Tomorrow will strike out again in winters white lands

Thinking it will not be long hopefully before seeing spring again!

Angel Wing Songs

Trees wave with the gentle breeze

Wind whispers as the angels wings

 Move through the branches

Tinkling sounds of the wind chimes

 As the angels swiftly fly

Like the speed of light

Chimes swirl, creating magical sounds

The music of nature, the whispering winds

From the angels wings

Soft, light, flowing

Feathers encourages the songs of birds

Bees buzzing intensely

 Among the swaying flowers

The background sounds of the orchestra

Is the blended creation music for nature's serenity

Angels conducting performances

Wrap around comfort

For all to assist and accompany them

As the winds whisper angel wing songs

Feelings of peaceful serene happiness

Engulfs one's heart

For the love of more songs

Created by

The angel wings in nature

Who Are You?

Are you the woman you want to be?

Making choices to live your dream

Or pleasing others whims it seems

Are you being that woman of passion?

Making choices that make you happy

Are you living a life that clouds your heart?

Are you loved, respected each and every day?

Do you still carry a song in your heart?

Is your smile real or do you wear a mask?

Did you lose the woman you were in the past?

You are a woman that can do anything!

Put on your coat of armour

Demand what you need!

Be the woman you want to be!

Life goes by quickly

So love each and everyday

Following your passions and your dreams

It is hard to make changes but you can make changes

Woman are always pleasing others

We cannot change the world

Be the woman you want to be!

Love who you are!

When you look in the mirror

Make the changes in you

So you know who you are!

Written in dedication to women giving them courage and strength to change their lives

Wind Whisper Journey

My years of life's hearts whispers

Including present and past

It was a love venture right from my heart

To share my life with you!

Included is many lessons of unhappiness and grief

But also the hope attained while living through each stage

What it brought to my life

The strength and courage attained

From heart aches and strife

The love of nature included

The Lord helped me through

To come to my place in present

That I have journeyed to

I am grateful for each day I have

To pick up my pen again

Let my emotions run freely

On a page honest and carefree

While the words flow on each page

The many whispers that I have to share

The gift that if we wake up each day

It is a blessing and a gift itself

Never give up hope do to fear

Do not fear death when your time comes

This is not the only place

This is not the end!

Keep your head up knowing each day

Your loved ones are with you

Each step of the way

We do have our hearts broken

In this journey in life's path

The whisper will help you get to the place

Maybe help you get through

In my many poems you will see

My life changed in many ways

It changed over the years from a to z

If you learned a little something

Made your heart feel some love in short!

Then I accomplished with my whispers

My life goal from my whispers art

Learn from each wind whisper

Be kind to everyone you meet

Love the Lord above

Enjoy nature and wildlife

That is a drive from your front door

Be thankful for your many blessings

Include forgiveness, love and laughter

On your path in life

You will have many whispers

That will guide you in your life

Do not be afraid when it is over

We might meet at Heaven's gate

Until then keep learning and growing

I might never meet you in person

When my time is over here

Look me up in heaven

I will be writing up there!

Do not be afraid of tomorrow

Tomorrow might never come

Be kind and honest

Reach out a helping hand!

If you make a choice on your journey

Think of the wind whisper it creates

Wind whispers are things we learn

Through years of life!

Take this love I have passed to you

If you have felt or learned anything

Pass this book of whispers on

Give hope and love to each person

You pass it to!

The world is a big place

If I can touch many hearts

With my words I need to share

Love can touch so many hearts

Hopefully before my life is over

I shared many wind whispers

With love from my writing whispers art!

Time Is

A moment

A smile

A word

A memory

Time is a gift

Time is now!

Time is a minute

Time is an hour

Time is months and years

Time is now!

Time is life each second

Each day

Each moment and memory

Make your life count!

Your time is now!

I wrote this to remind us that we must not take life for granted. We need to take each day as a gift it is just that a gift. I have loved so many people that wanted just one more day!

Wind Whispers Finale

Wind Whispers

Is a collection of poems based from my own personal journey in life.

These poems contain the heart ache and strife I have lived through. Taking one day at a time! I asked you to take my hand and walk with me and open your heart. In this book my heart filled emotions I opened up to you. My trials have been many as you have read with faith and courage I look forward now to tomorrow whatever it gives me! I also look for the messages that are sent to me from my many loved ones that are gone. I see feathers, coins and hear their favorite songs. This was part of my tapestry of life that I have shared with you. If anything I hope you take away the fact that you are never alone. After opening my heart I have come to know that wherever we live on God's green earth I continue to look forward to tomorrow and the lessons it will teach me. My loved ones are in heaven still watching over me. I continue to have courage to help others in their crosses that they carry. I ask you to let God or your Higher Power hold your hand from here. You are a beautiful person that has special gifts to be shared with the world. Some of our life's lessons are painful never give up hope. Hope is that special something that we have when nothing else has worked. I am giving you hope right now!

Understand that your loved ones are always with you. If you have a son or daughter that is addicted to drugs or alcohol don't give up on them they will find their way! Lend your helping hand to someone else on their life journey once you find your way. This life it is about helping yourself and others along the way! I believe in you! Tomorrow is a new day!

I hope you enjoyed reading my poetic path of my life's whispers!

May a piece of heaven be with you I know it is!

Blessings,
Debbie

AUTHOR BIOGRAPHY

Debra Quigley was born in Peterborough Ontario. She is the Mother of two sons and has one Granddaughter. Her profession is working with seniors as a Personal Support Worker. She loves writing poetry from her heart. Her poetry is simple and real! She writes touching hearts one reader one heart at a time. She returned to her little piece of heaven to live again in the small country hamlet. Debra loves nature, growing vegetables and campfires. She contributed in Spiritual Writers Network publications *Touched by an Angel, The Best of 2013* and *Whispers of the Soul*. She also contributes poetry in New Age News Magazine. Debra plans to have her next book, a memoir, published in 2015 that she currently is working on. If you wish to contact Debra her email is debbiequigley2001@hotmail.com if you wish to comment on this publication.

This book is dedicated to all that I have loved and lost thus far on my journey.

Family and friends that supported me opening my heart on this venture giving hope to others.

Thank you to Shanda Trofe, creator of Spiritual Writers Network for believing in my whispering art of poetry.

Made in the USA
Charleston, SC
17 October 2014